BAD WORDS
An Illustrated Book of C

Poems by Dean

With artwork by:

Dean Beattie, Warwick Johnson-Cadwell, Mike Norton,
Luke Parker, Hatch, Alex Riegel, Gustaffo Vargas, Ewan,
Joe DellaGatta, Dimitris Pantazis, Mr Hope,
Heidi Burton, Nathan Stell, Ben McSweeney, Olli Hihnala and
Baldemar Rivas.

Design assist by Calum Lester

CONTENTS
A poem about:

Any illustrations not listed above are by Dean Beattie

Dear Tom

The fact that you are reading this
Means that I am now dead
And now that I'm beyond your reach
I've things that must be said

You know your car got scratched that time?
I did that with a key
And when your bike got stolen...
Well....that was also me

I smashed your downstairs windows
Set fire to your van
Spread rumours that your wife was sleeping...
With another man

I got you sacked from your last job
And dyed your son's hair blue
I kidnapped, killed and cooked your dog
And ate him in a stew

I pushed poo through your letter box
Poured poison in your pond
And now I've sent this letter
To torment you...from beyond

I hope this letter kills you, Tom
That would be sublime
The perfect ending to all this
To screw you - one last time

Best wishes

Derek

EAT SHIT.

1.

I met him in a chat room
Where our fantasies aligned
This man agreed to lots of things
That others had declined

We shared a dream of eating
So we struck a solid deal
I would be the diner
He would be my human meal

This isn't my house
I don't have a key
But I don't give a fuck
I'm a burglar, y'see?

Dorothy thought that it was quite bizarre
to spend Friday night in the boot of a car

The gimp mask and handcuffs were also frustrating
but this stuff can happen with internet dating

6 steps left, then 3 feet down
That's where you'll find **Joanna Brown**

4 steps right and 2 steps back
Dig there to see **Belinda Black**

5 steps forward, 5 steps right
I know that one's **Amanda White**

3 steps backwards, 1 left, I think..
Yes, ... that one's name was **Wendy Pink**

Today I'm getting married
To a guy from Pakistan
I really can't recall his name
But he seems a **lovely** man

Weddings are exciting
But not this time, I fear
The law is bound to stop me soon
It's my fifteenth one this year

My nickname's **'Green Card Debbie'**
And I'm known round here, ya see
Immigration Marriage Fraud
For a reasonable fee

Want somebody murdered?
Yes? Then I'm the man you need!
For just two thousand British pounds
I'll do the deadly deed

I'll strangle, shoot or stab for you
Electrocute or freeze
I'll bludgeon, burn or poison
Or I'll hang people from trees

I'll throw 'em down a lift shaft
Decapitate or flay
I'll deep-fry, starve or mummify
Or.....just let them decay

I'll suffocate or drown 'em
I'll dehydrate or bleed
I'll feed them to my hungry dogs
Satisfaction guaranteed

The hammer sat uneasily beneath the dirt –
waiting nervously for the day it would be discovered
...by a random dog-walker

Things that were stolen during the break-in:

Nothing. I faked the break in.

Things that I told the insurance company were
stolen during the break-in:

TV
Laptop
Mobile phone
Vintage record player
Cat
Very, very realistic Russian sex doll

My heartbeat's going mental
But I'm trying to look chilled
I've got some cocaine up my bum
I'm absolutely filled

The customs guy is eyeing me
I need to hide my fear
It's hard though -
Cos I think he knows
There's drugs stuck in my rear

If I can make it past his gaze
If I can keep my cool
I'll earn myself 2 thousand pounds
For acting as a mule

I don't think there's a sniffer dog
But if there is - I'll fail
One whiff of what's lodged in my butt
And I'll be off to jail

Come on now. Let's be positive.
I'll get paid what I'm owed
Soon I'll be home
And pooping out

This valuable load

I've found that people like me
but I really don't know why
After all, I like to steal stuff
and I almost always lie

I blackmail when I get the chance
I scam, plot and conspire
I'm also quite the vandal
and I love to play with fire

I've got a pretty face though
so that might just play a part -
in the fact that no-one seems to see
my cruel and blackened heart

16.

My mind is telling me this is a bad idea and that I should turn and run - but my stupidity overrides the warning.

The ground beneath my feet is muddy and wild - making each footstep a perilous chore.

Shoes are fucking ruined.

Toes are cold.

The dark, heavy door that stands ahead scowls grimly at me - but its defiance is undermined by wood rot and rusty hinges.

Resigned to failure, it opens at the slightest push.

The door can eat shit.

I'm inside.

I've never forgotten the smell of this place.

Dampness and foreboding.

Piss. Hatred.

Bleach.

I remember the mouldy walls.

The mouldy walls remember me.

They whisper my name.

They tell me to leave.

They tell me they've seen enough.

REMOVE HIS SHIRT
REMOVE HIS VEST
CARVE MY NAME
INTO HIS CHEST

'Am I dead?'
His victim said
'Not yet,'
Said Edward Peck

Then curled his lip
Increased his grip
And snapped her pale, white neck

I THOUGHT IT MUST BE REALLY COOL
TO BE A MAN LIKE **YOU**
SO **I** STOLE YOUR IDENTITY
AND NOW **I** AM **YOU** TOO

'Did his wife know?' people asked
'She MUST have done,' they said
'Or had a strong suspicion rolling round inside her head.'

'I think she's EVIL,' people spat
'She told him what to do'
'Or planted ideas in his head then watched them slowly brew.'

'She's standing by him, dont'cha know?'
'He's innocent,' she said
She still insists the claims are false and that we've been misled.

'Misled my arse!', the people hissed
'She's telling bloody lies!'
'He did those things - AND MORE!' they said
'The guilt's there in his eyes!'

'Lock him up!' the people cried
And SHE deserves the same!
HE may have done those horrid things but SHE'S as much to blame!

I roll the little, metal wheel with my thumb - and ignition is instant.
It's only a cheap lighter -
but the flame it creates is as beautiful as any other.

I stare at it for a second - then close my eyes to enjoy the white ghost
it's burnt into my retina.
A small pleasure before the main event.

I'm doing a dustbin in the park today.

Some might say it's an easy target, - but they don't see what I see.
A cast iron box of opportunity -
full of perfect combustibles and endless promise.

Atop the pile, a discarded newspaper sits provocatively -
and its crisp, dry pages whisper encouragement that I have no
intention of resisting.

I embrace the inevitable and extend my arm gently -
allowing the tiny fire in my hand to kiss its seducer.

A thin trail of smoke appears immediately -
and, as I inhale the thickening air, my heart quickens.

I savour the moment -
but know only too well that it's already time to leave.

I'll watch the blaze flourish from afar -
but people can never know it was mine.

They just wouldn't understand.

24.

The most horrific version of me is waiting patiently below a thin veneer of normality

Olivia watched the report on TV
It said that her husband would soon be set free
Her revenge was all plotted and premeditated
She'd feel gratified when he'd been **castrated**

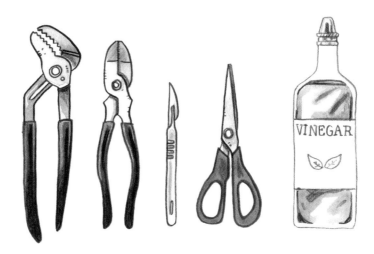

I ain't dun nuffink' wrong, y'know?
I ain't dun nuffink' bad
Juss sold a bit a weed an' dat
Dat judge woz fuckin' mad

6 years, I got. 6 fuckin' years
For sellin' weed an' coke
Tha justice fuckin' system
Is a total fuckin' joke

A bit a' coke - a bit a' crack
And yeah, I stabbed dat guy
But dat weren't all dat bad, y'know
He didn't even die

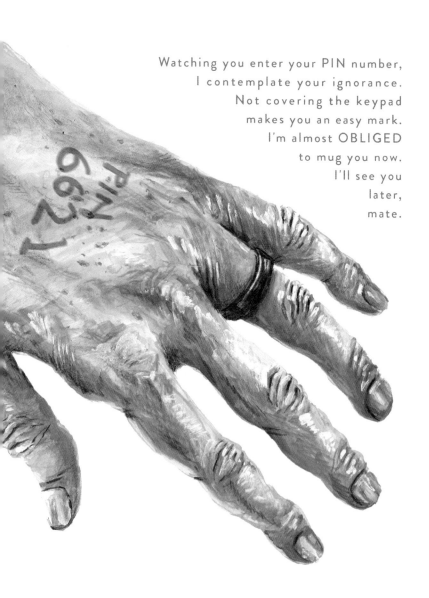

Watching you enter your PIN number,
I contemplate your ignorance.
Not covering the keypad
makes you an easy mark.
I'm almost OBLIGED
to mug you now.
I'll see you
later,
mate.

THE OTHERS USED TO BULLY HER

REVENGE WAS ON HER MIND

THOSE BASTARDS WOULD ALL HAVE TO PAY

FOR BEING SO UNKIND

There was NOT a grain of truth
In anything she said
Her husband WASN'T in New York
He was, in fact, quite dead

Her mother WASN'T travelling
Her dad? NOT on a cruise
She'd coldly murdered all of them...
...but left too many clues

Detectives dug in her back yard
And found what she had done
They asked her why she'd killed them all
She giggled... 'just for fun.'

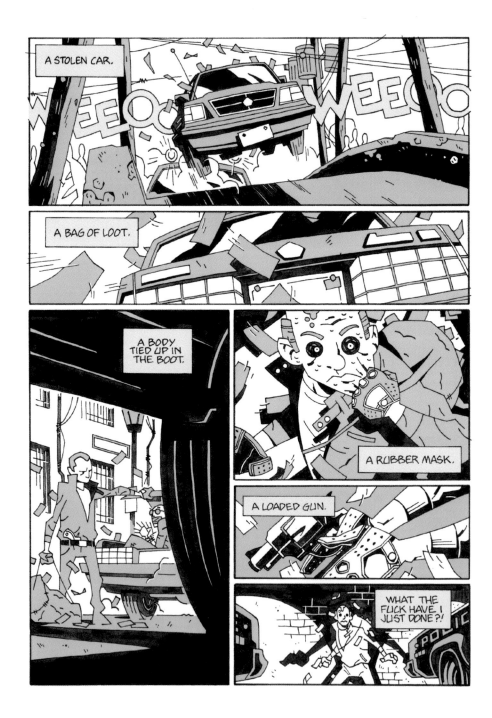

I got some stuff here yesterday
And now I'm back for more
I never pay for anything
When I'm in this store

I just find the stuff I want
And then I steal that shit
I slide it all into my bag
Until no more will fit

I don't get caught that often
And I don't care when I do
The shop won't ever prosecute
They haven't got a clue

They'll just slap me on the wrist
Or give me 'strong advice'
So I'll just keep on stealing
And I'll never pay the price

He's Roberto - I am John
and we're here to inspire...
...you to pay a bit of 'special tax'
So you don't have a fire

This place looks quite delightful
and I think you would regret
Passing up our little offer
And not honouring your debt

Now, I can't see the future
but think if you fail to pay
You might see some misfortune,
pain and sadness come your way

Three hundred quid should sort it out
and buy the guarantee
Of a month's worth of protection
from Roberto - and from me

I watch you as you leave your house
I watch you lock your door
I watch you walk your garden path
I've watched all this before

I watch you get into your car
I watch you pull away
I watch you sit in traffic
Like I watch you every day

I watch you park up in the town
I watch you board the train
I watch you take your usual seat
I sit nearby again

I watch you as you read your book
I watch you check your phone
I watch you as the others leave
Once more, we are alone

I watch you try to not see me
I watch you fight the tide
I watch you hide the yearning
That you've always had inside

One day you'll fall into my arms
One day you'll not ignore
Til then I will watch patiently
Your fan – forevermore

His basic lack of money
Meant he couldn't buy the things
That he thought would make him happy
So he stole some diamond rings

He stole a silver bracelet too
A laptop and a car
Then when he stole a jumbo jet
He knew he'd gone too far

I just found a hand in my garden
A man's hand - of that I am sure
Cos it's quite big and overly hairy
And in need of a good manicure

I presume it's attached to a body
Which is hidden there under the ground
Providing compost for my roses
Which now thrive on this burial mound

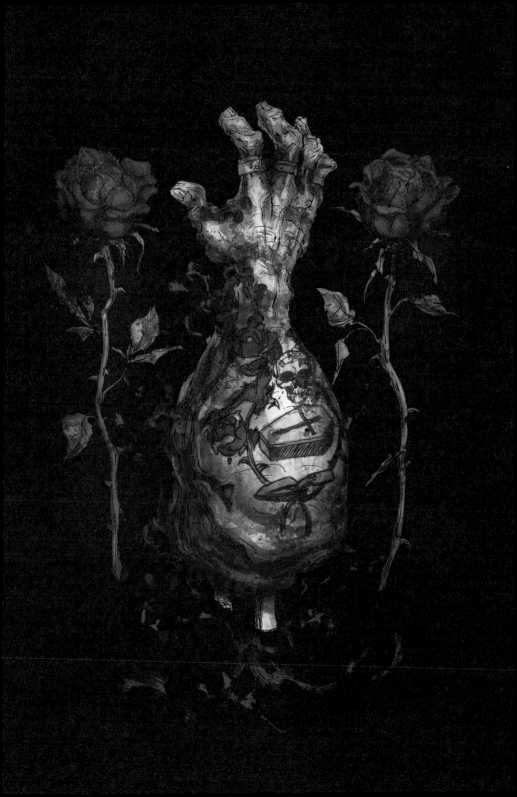

He waved the gun in my face and demanded that I give him all the money from the till

I said 'say please'

He shot me in the arm

I opened the till and gave him everything he wanted

He said 'thank you'

I said 'ah, so you DO have some manners!'

He shot me in the arm again and then left the store

I'm taking it as a moral victory

I paid for my lunch with a bank note
A bank note I knew was a fake
The guilt has been driving me mental
My dishonesty was a mistake

And whilst I am making confessions
I need to tell you about Mike
The man I keep locked in my basement
And torture whenever I like

My God! What a weight off my shoulders!
I'd crippled myself with regret!
That bank note thing made me feel awful
But now I can start to forget

In '62
I robbed a train
Then ran away to sunny Spain

I live like a king
And drink champagne
But yearn to see my home again

The moment he saw her face..........

he knew he had to cut it off and wear it as a mask

My eyelids seem to weigh a ton -

but I open them defiantly and, for a brief second,

see the blurred outline of a woman I think I know.

Anxiety and nausea strike in unison - and are joined quickly

by a violent maelstrom of panicked thoughts.

Did she drug me?

Is she going to cut my nob off?

Am I going to die?

If I die - will I shit my pants?

Who's going to find my body?

Will they be disgusted by all the shit?

There is no escaping this.

My limbs are cold and dead. My heart beats frantically.

I can offer no resistance to the punishment I'm about to receive.

This ridiculous drama happens EVERY time I forget our anniversary.

He spoke the words decisively
and dealt the chilling blow
'Insufficient evidence'
'You are now free to go'

She turned her head and smirked at me
then gestured something crude
My lawyer shrugged his shoulders
with a practised attitude

The injustice cut into my soul
I called the judge a twat
The judge then held me in contempt
I wasn't havin' that

I leapt up from the wooden bench
and shouted 'fuck you all!!'
Security then tackled me
and pinned me to the wall

They forced my arm behind my back
and then the fight was done
They'd bested me two times that day
The law had truly won

When I was young
I done sum fings
That weren't that bloody clever

The kinda fings
That are so bad
They haunt ya dreams forever

Hello, my most respected sir
I write to you this day
With a secret opportunity
We must not now delay

My name is Mr William
And this chance I offer you
Is really most incredible
But definitely true

I will put the tidy sum
Of 15 million pounds
Directly in your bank account
Now tell me how that sounds?

I want to give you money
But first will need your aid
I promise you, most treasured friend
You're going to get paid

The source of all this money
Is a man who's now deceased
And there are certain steps to take
To see the cash released

First I need your sort code
And your address
And your pin
The number on your credit card
Name of your next of kin
I'll need to know your passwords
For your email and your banks
Your 8 digit account code
And that's it, my friend
Much thanks

Sir, you must act quickly
Or the bank will gain control!
This project is our secret, friend!
You cannot tell a soul!

This estate is fuckin' grim
The tenants are all rough
They all smoke crack and fight an' that
I've had E...fuckin...nuff.

I'm gonna start to kill a few
Eradicate the scum
Cleanse the fuckin' gene pool
BEGINNIN' WIV YOUR MUM

His drawings detailed his predictions

The things that he claimed would come true

An electric chair showed how he said HE would die

A sword - how he planned to kill **YOU**

I THINK IT'S BEST – THAT YOU DON'T SEE
THE FIERCE BLUR WHERE MY FACE SHOULD BE
THE HATRED THAT I FEEL FOR THEE
AVERT YOUR EYES! DON'T LOOK AT ME!

He told me to give him my phone
I said 'no'
He told me he'd stab me
I gave him my phone

He told me to give him my wallet
I said 'no'
He told me he'd stab me
I gave him my wallet

He told me to give him my coat
I said 'no'
He said he'd stab me
I said 'But that will ruin the coat'

I made my escape whilst he pondered the dilemma

He called her ANGEL
She called him ARSEHOLE

Their future looked like SHIT

I started due to necessity

But necessity has transformed into a greedy addiction

The greedy addiction fills me with shame

But that shame is subdued by my innate sense of self preservation

Self preservation keeps me alive

But MY life has become a series of spiralling rash acts

Rash acts will get me caught

But maybe getting caught would be best

Her hands clenched tight

and turned to fists

Her hatred filled the air

He cowered down before her

She rejoiced at his **despair**

'Am I safe?'

she gently cried

'Of course you are,'

he calmly lied

WE BOTH KNOW WHY YOU WENT TO LEEDS

WE BOTH KNOW WHAT YOU DID

WE BOTH KNOW WHAT YOU TOLD YOUR WIFE

WE BOTH KNOW WHAT YOU HID

WE BOTH KNOW WHAT COULD HAPPEN NEXT

WE BOTH KNOW YOU SHOULD PAY

WE BOTH KNOW I COULD TELL YOUR WIFE

WE BOTH KNOW WHAT I'D SAY

WE BOTH KNOW I COULD RUIN YOU

WE BOTH KNOW I DON'T CARE

WE BOTH KNOW THIS IS BLACKMAIL

THAT'S THE PRICE OF YOUR AFFAIR

Comin' in the pub an' drinkin' those fuckin' energy drinks an' wearin' their hooded fuckin' tops.

Bangin' on bout how they're bein' disrespected by everybody - an' arguin' out loud on their stupid little phones.

I'd have slashed the fuckers to death 60 years ago.

Set their feet in concrete. Thrown 'em in the canal or set fire to 'em in the fuckin' woods.

Yeah, I used to be someone round 'ere.

The girls ain't no better.

Fuckin' stupid orange faces an' eyebrows drawn on with thick, black fuckin' pens. Drinkin' pints of lager and big fuckin' jugs of neon-lookin' shit that stains their mouths blue. They shout an' swear an' fight each other in the streets an' pass out in the gutter.

I'd 'a sorted 'em out 60 years ago.

A good fuckin' slappin' would 'a done it.

Else I'd 'a carved 'em up an' left 'em outside their parents' house.

Yeah, I used to be someone round 'ere.

My drivin' is **impeccable**
I'm super as can be
Those 14 pints of lager
Have had **no effect** on me

Soon, my love
You'll slip away
And I will hold you tight

I'll watch the life
depart your eyes
as you give up the fight

The tattoos he wore on his body
recorded the things he had done
His left arm showed liquor and women
His right arm - a dagger and gun

His knuckles each carried a letter
and spelled out the words 'love' and 'hate'
He used one to flirt with the ladies
The other - to intimidate

His chest was emblazoned with faces
Of people who'd 'ended up dead'
His friends were all drawn in bright emerald green
His enemies - deep crimson red

His back was adorned with the big Pearly Gates
Saint Peter and angels as well
He'd convinced himself he'd go to heaven
The truth - he was destined for hell

They came in through the window
It's been smashed
They used a rock
Looks like they tried the door before
But struggled with the lock

There's mud there - where they entered
And some footprints
'bout size 10
That tells me that the criminals
Are likely to be men

Their trail leads to the kitchen
Open cupboards
Lots of mess
Don't know what they were looking for
Some food .....or drink, ...I guess?

They then went to the bedroom
Wardrobes ransacked
Jewellery found
They've thrown the victim's clothes and stuff
All over the ground

And their fight began here -- in this room
There's blood
It's everywhere
The burglars must have disagreed
About how best to share

No bodies in the house though
So they lived
And got away
But not for long, I'd like to think
........We've got their DNA

I DON'T KNOW QUITE WHAT SET HIM OFF
BUT IT ESCALATED FAST
HE BARED HIS TEETH
AND SMASHED HIS PINT

THEN SOMEBODY GOT GLASSED

I've just made you a cup of tea
Best drink it while it's hot
You want some biscuits on a plate?
I'll go see what I've got

What's that now?
You're feeling ill?
Don't worry, you'll be fine
Your tea tastes kind of funny, eh?
Well it's just the same as mine

Oh, except I poisoned yours
With arsenic, nonetheless
Give it 15 minutes
And you'll be a bloody mess

Yes, he looks all innocent
And yes, he's only young
But, if you mess with Alfie
He will hang you by your tongue

What's that? You think I'm joking?
Well, just go ahead and see
Break his toys or steal his bike
But rather you than me

He won't give you a warning, mate
He'll go straight for your knees
He's only got his milk teeth
But he'll chew through you with ease

Then, once he's got you at a height
Where he can reach your face
He'll punch you squarely on the nose
and spray your eyes with mace

At that stage you'll be helpless
And he'll leave you laying there
To reflect upon your actions
And relive the whole nightmare

At this point, I hope you believe me
I know that it sounds pretty wild
But my last word on this, as I leave you, my friend
Is PLEASE! Do NOT fuck with this child!

PRISON WARDEN:

Andy Lanning

HEAD PRISON GUARD:

Monica Golding

PRISON GUARDS:

Jimmy Furlong
Grainne O'Brien
Rocky Lee
Aditya Desai
Marc Rouleau
James Lawrence
Debbie Auld
Hazel Tatlow
Simone Guglielmini
Mike Cassella
Andi Rensen Aguion

FORENSIC PSYCHOLOGISTS:

Paul Castle
Nate Lovett

SUBSTANCE ABUSE COUNCILLORS:

Dave West
Adam Robert Wyman

ART THERAPIST:

Andy W Clift

MUSIC THERAPIST:

Stephen Press

PRISON CHAPLAIN:

Steve Tanner

PRISON COOK:

James Corcoran

LIBRARIAN:

Elizabeth U

INMATES:

Mark Seddon
Richard Williams
B.E. Murer
Heidi Burton
Sarah Stell
Kirk Spencer
Gary Crutchley
Madcat Angrymog
Jon Cottrell
Colin Bell
Kai Holmstrom
Jay
Ching-Ho Lee
Bud
Death By Heroism
John Kerecz
Martin Simmonds
Fraser Campbell
Norman Hardy
Richard Archer
Jim Barton
Nathan
Pete Woods
Matt Rooke
Russell Ludwin
jstudlystevens
Jamie Gambell
Terri Harvey
Asa Wheatley
Geoff Martin
Charlotte Smith
Daniel Matless
Brendan Cullen
Aaron Heisler
Wendy Gilbert
Steve Offenheim
Josh Abraham
Lucas Devine
Rodney Smith
Backerkit
Θοδωρής Καγιάντας

MAXIMUM SECURITY WING:

Alan Purdie
Kirk Moore
Eben E. B. Burgoon
Tom Charlesworth
Kara Morgan
Ken Reynolds
Jay Nystrom
Lewis Moss
Gibson Grey
James Pollard
Blanche Brier
Stephanie Bertsch

SOLITARY CONFINEMENT:

Nick Gribbon
Sarah Harris
Chief Stride
Daniel Kinnill
Paul T. Davies
Kaci Johnston

DEATH ROW INMATES:

Jay Eales
Michael Conde
Peter Seddon
Dimitris Pantazis
Jason Quinlan
Olli Hihnala